GUNS
AND THE
#NEVER AGAIN
MOVEMENT

WHAT WOULD IT TAKE TO END MASS SHOOTINGS?

Emma Carlson Berne

Content Consultant:
Meg Heckman, Assistant Professor,
Northeastern University School of Journalism

COMPASS POINT BOOKS
a capstone imprint

Compass Point Books are published by Capstone
1710 Roe Crest Drive, North Mankato, Minnesota 56003
www.capstonepub.com

Editorial Credits
Michelle Bisson, editor; Sarah Bennett, designer; Kelly Garvin, media researcher; Katy LaVigne, production specialist

Photo Credits
Alamy/ZUMA Press, Inc, 28; Getty Images/AFP/LOREN ELLIOTT, 37; iStockphoto/ SolStock, 51; Newscom: @ParisaMichelle/SplashNews, 47, ABA, 43, GARY I ROTHSTEIN/UPI, 7, Gary W. Greens, TNS, 55, GEORGE FREY/REUTERS, 20, JEFF MITCHELL/REUTERS, 11, MIKE HASKEY/KRT, 29, Mike Stocker, TNS, 5, Richard Watson UPI Photo Service, 19; North Wind Picture Archive, 16; Shutterstock: a katz, 36, Anatoly Vartanov, 33, Dom Ernest L Gomez, 12, Draftfolio, 39, GagliardPhotography, 30, Gina Jacobs, 24, Hayk_Shalunts, 46, John T Takai, 52, Kate Way, 34, KelseyJ, 14, 21, KMH Photovideo, 41, laura.h, 35 (bottom), LIghtspring, 31, Makyzz, 56, ND700, 18, Nicole S Glass, 44-45, Rob Crandall, 42, Robert Biedermann, 9, rodimov, 35 (top), Roman Sotola, 39, Ryan Rodrick Beller, 17, SFerdon, cover, TFoxFoto, 23, WKanadpon, 32

Artistic elements: Shutterstock/Kozhadub Sergei

Library of Congress Cataloging-in-Publication Data
Names: Berne, Emma Carlson, author.
Title: Guns and the #neveragain movement : what would it take to end mass shooting? / by Emma Carlson Berne.
Description: North Mankato, Minnesota : Compass Point Books, [2019] | Series: Schools, guns and mass shootings | Audience: Grade 4 to 6.
Identifiers: LCCN 2019004992| ISBN 9780756561727 (hardcover) | ISBN 9780756562274 (pbk.) | ISBN 9780756561949 (ebook pdf)
Subjects: LCSH: Mass shootings—United States—Juvenile literature. | Violent crimes—United States—Juvenile literature. | Gun control—United States—Juvenile literature. | Firearms ownership—Government policy—United States—Juvenile literature.
Classification: LCC HV7436 .B476 2019 | DDC 363.3300973—dc23
LC record available at https://lccn.loc.gov/2019004992

Printed and bound in the United States of America.
PA71

Table of Contents

CHAPTER ONE

Schools, Guns, and
Mass Shootings

I've never had a great memory, but I can recall each detail we saw in the hallway during our escape. . . . It was carnage. There were bullet holes everywhere. Blood covered and stained the floor, and all of us got blood on our shoes. There was a girl lying facedown in front of the girls' bathroom, right next to our door. . . .

Augustus Griffith Jr., survivor of the
Marjory Stoneman Douglas High School shooting

In 2018 Augustus Griffith Jr. was a student at Marjory Stoneman Douglas (MSD) High School in Parkland, Florida. On February 14, he also became something else: a survivor of a school shooting.

Nikolas Cruz, an 18-year-old former student at MSD, entered the building and, using an AR-15 semiautomatic assault rifle he had bought legally, shot and killed 17 people. Cruz was only one of many gunmen who have entered public spaces, including schools, churches, clubs, and restaurants, and shot and killed many people. Griffith was only one of many survivors. Often the shooters who commit mass violence at schools are teenagers themselves. They are kids shooting other kids. *Active shooter* is a term that most people recognize now. An active shooter is generally defined as someone who enters a confined space full of people and shoots them at random, with no real pattern or method to the shooting.

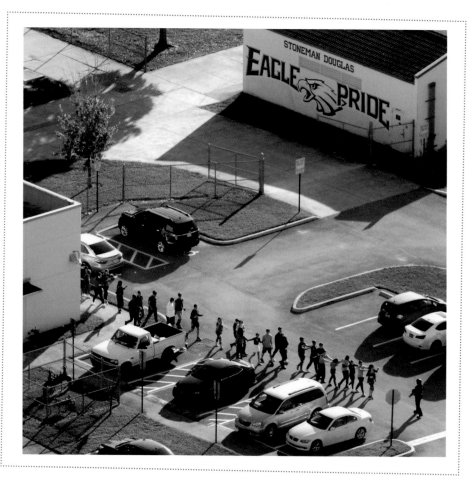

Survivors of the Parkland high school shooting were evacuated after it was safe to do so.

What counts as a mass shooting?

Shootings such as the one at MSD are also called mass shootings. Researchers and journalists disagree on how to define a mass shooting as opposed to other types of gun violence. Generally a mass shooting is one in which multiple people are shot, usually in a single location. The victim and the shooter are not involved with a gang situation, organized crime, a domestic situation, or a drug deal. And, in the type of mass shooting discussed here, the shooters are not considered terrorists and their crimes are not considered acts of terrorism.

In the narrowest definition, terrorists commit random violence against civilians with a political or ideological aim. But this is not an easy distinction. The people who are in mass shootings definitely feel terror. And sometimes the motivations of the mass shooters aren't known. Many have argued that labeling a shooting an act of terrorism can be a way of expressing prejudice, especially against Muslims. They also argue that people are too quick to label a mass shooting "terrorism" or "not terrorism," without exploring the details. But in general, the incidents discussed here are those that were not labled as terrorism by analysts and the news media. Still it is important to point out that the news media express a white, middle-class point of view. Many people consider racially motivated shootings to be a form of terrorism and argue that they should be classified as such.

Guns have been a part of the United States since the very first days of the nation. But according to a 2014 FBI study, active shooting situations are on the rise. In fact, by the FBI's definition, they have increased at an average rate of 16 percent each year between 2000 and 2013. There were an average of 6.4 shootings per year during the first seven years of the study, and 16.4 shootings per year during the last seven years.

But others disagree that mass shootings are on the rise. Researcher Grant Duwe calculates the frequency of mass shootings according to the increase in the U.S. population over time. He argues that the frequency of mass shootings has remained fairly steady since the 1970s. However, Duwe also states that mass shootings have gotten more deadly, with more people now killed per incident.

No matter which way you slice the statistics or fiddle with the definitions, one thing is clear: Mass shootings are violent, traumatic, and heartbreaking. They are a national problem and a national argument.

Mourners pay their respects to the Marjory Stoneman Douglas shooting victims.

Americans and Their Guns

But haven't Americans always had guns? If guns have always been a part of American life, why are mass shootings a new problem?

They aren't new—by guns or other weapons. Our country has had mass killings at least as far back as 1927, when Andrew Kehoe, a local farmer, detonated 1,000 pounds of dynamite he'd hidden in the basement of a school in Bath Township, Michigan. Forty-five people died, including 38 children and Kehoe himself.

In 1966 a man named Charles Whitman shot down 14 people at random from his perch in the clock tower at the University of Texas-Austin. Whitman was an Eagle Scout and a former Marine sniper.

What characterizes mass shootings in more recent years is their frequency and deadliness. The U.S. has more mass shootings than any other nation. Between 1966 and 2012 there were 292 incidents around the world in which four or more people were killed. Of those, 90 happened in the U.S. That means that while only about 5 percent of the world's population lives in the U.S., the nation has about 31 percent of all the mass shootings. The five deadliest shootings in U.S. history—the most people killed at a time—occurred between 2007 and 2018.

Mass shootings do not fall under one easy definition. Some argue that four or more people must be killed in order for a shooting to become a "mass shooting." But in general, the mass shootings discussed here are of two types. In one, a shooter enters a confined place, like a school, business, church, or synagogue. In the other, the killer enters a populated outdoor space, like a park, and

Five of the deadliest shootings in the United States from 1949 to 2018 have taken place from 2007 to 2018.

1. October 1, 2017, Las Vegas, Nevada: 58 killed
2. June 12, 2016, Orlando, Florida: 49 killed
3. April 16, 2007, Blacksburg, Virginia: 32 killed
4. December 14, 2012, Newtown, Connecticut: 27 killed
5. November 5, 2017, Sutherland Springs, Texas: 26 killed

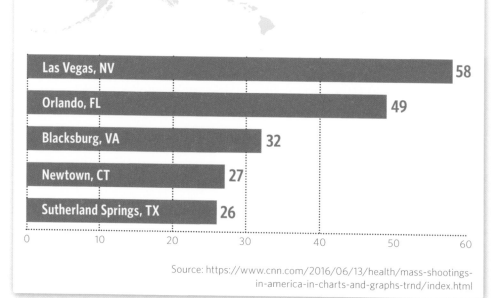

Source: https://www.cnn.com/2016/06/13/health/mass-shootings-in-america-in-charts-and-graphs-trnd/index.html

begins shooting at random, killing multiple people. In neither type of shooting is there a previous connection to drugs, organized crime, or family disputes.

Sometimes a shooter will use a semiautomatic or assault-style weapon that can fire many rounds of ammunition. Sometimes shooters will commit suicide with their own weapons before they can be caught by police. Most of the time, the shooters are men. An FBI study of active shooter incidents between 2000 and 2013 found that fewer than 4 percent of the shooters were women. And those who commit school shootings and other types of mass shootings tend to be white. Their motivations vary but the shooters often show no signs of mental illness in the days before the attacks. They usually have a grudge or grievance against the group they are shooting. Sometimes they are motivated by racial hatred. Some see themselves as heroes.

The Effects of Columbine

On April 20, 1999, Eric Harris, 18, and Dylan Klebold, 17, opened fire on their teachers and classmates at Columbine High School in Littleton, Colorado. By the time they were done, they had killed 13 people and wounded more than 20 others. Then they killed themselves in the school library. Twenty years later, the shooting is often simply called "Columbine." It is still considered one of the worst school shootings in American history. Columbine was not the beginning of mass shootings in schools, but

Mourners gathered together for solace in the aftermath of the Columbine High School shooting.

it has a place as a beginning in the public consciousness. Random mass school shootings were happening, and they were not going away.

There is no form of gun violence that is not important. Anticipating each situation spawns unique fear in the members of the group that might be affected. For example, African American parents might fear for the lives of their young children. People who live in areas with heavy drug traffic might worry about being caught in crossfire. And children and adults of all backgrounds, social classes, regions, and races fear mass shootings. There is something about the randomness, the suddenness, and the deadliness that combine to make a fear stew. Because of this fear, Americans have launched into a national debate about how to control these shootings. The debate is emotional and intense. And it is ongoing.

"I'll Never Forget His Pleas"
A School Shooting Survivor Remembers

In a book written by survivors of the Marjory Stoneman Douglas High shooting, Augustus Griffith Jr. remembers that day:

"A single loud bang emerged from the stairwell down the hall and resonated throughout the school. . . . [Our teacher] shoved his heavy wooden desk in front of the door. . . . The bangs grew nearer, louder, and faster. We heard screams. We heard cries and pleas. Silencing them with an unmatched volume and intensity, gunshots. They were right outside our door.

"A student screamed outside. He was pleading for help and sanctuary. I'll never forget his pleas. The shots stopped eventually, introducing us to a piercing silence, soon followed by wailing sirens outside. The student in the hallway was still begging to be saved. . . . He knocked on our door, still screaming for help. He continued to desperately attempt to open the locked door, knocking gravely and loudly. . . .

"Students [were] lying near the elevators. We walked into the stairwell. At the top of the stairs, there was another body.

"We exited the building from the side, and there was a bloodstain on the ground in front of the door, and more police officers than I had ever seen were standing in front of the building. . . . This was the work of a monster."

CHAPTER TWO

U.S. History,
U.S. Gun Laws

For the first time in my life, I called 911 from my phone and heard a woman's voice and tried to explain to her that I thought there was someone at our school shooting a gun. . . . During the course of my explanation at that time, the gunman was trying to come in. It was the most scared I've ever been in my life. I don't remember having the thought of, "I'm going to die." All I can remember thinking was, "I just can't believe that this is real."

Colin Goddard, survivor of the 2007 Virginia Tech shooting

Americans own a lot of guns. In fact, Americans own more guns than the citizens of any other country. They own 40 percent of all the guns in the world. Americans have approximately 400 million privately owned guns. That is enough to give every man, woman, and child in the

U.S. a gun and still have plenty left over. But that's not the case. These guns are actually all in the hands of an estimated 30 percent of the U.S. population.

In the U.S. the police, private security officers, and drivers of armored trucks that deliver money to and from banks are all armed with guns. This is expected. Almost any private citizen over the age of 18 or 21 (depending on the state they live in) can legally purchase a gun, with restrictions. In some states, private citizens can carry guns openly on their bodies or they can carry them in their cars.

Many in the U.S., including the people at the New Hampshire Gun Rally in March 2019, fear that gun control will restrict their rights.

The U.S. has some of the loosest gun laws in the industrialized world. In fact, for the most part, there is little national gun policy. Guns are primarily regulated state by state, which creates a sometimes confusing patchwork of laws. Most other industrialized countries have a unified national gun policy. In most states in the U.S., an average citizen can buy a gun in under an hour. Many states don't require a background check to see if the buyer has been convicted of a violent crime.

In many other industrialized and developing countries, civilians must go through a lengthy process involving eight to 10 steps before they can purchase a gun. In Germany, for instance, anyone who wants to buy a gun has to prove he or she needs the gun by joining a shooting club, getting a hunting license, or proving that his or her life is in danger. Then the person has to take a written and a physical test showing that he or she can handle a gun safely. Anyone under age 25 has to get a doctor's certificate saying he or she is mentally sound. The person must also have proper gun storage, which will be randomly checked by authorities. Then the person has to pass a background check. Then, and only then, can the person request a permit to buy a specific gun.

Guns in the U.S.

So why is the U.S. so different? Why do Americans have this love affair with guns? Many think it goes back to the Second Amendment to the Constitution, which states, "A well regulated Militia, being necessary to the security of a free State, the right of the people to keep and bear Arms, shall not be infringed." The Second Amendment is part of the Bill of Rights, which was ratified in 1791. At the time, it referred to state militias and their role in protecting the country from foreign invaders. Some say it was also about their role in keeping slaves from rebelling.

The founding fathers who wrote the Second Amendment were aware that governments would use soldiers to stop rebellions. Their main fear was of Britain, with whom they'd just fought a war for freedom. They also knew that they could lessen this risk by having a standing army only when fighting a war. The rest of the time state militias, made up of citizens who brought their own guns, could protect the country. The founding fathers were, in fact, in favor of gun control and had many laws restricting how and when firearms could be used. They required regular public inspections of guns, and even mandated that states to go door-to-door to note who had guns so that they could be easily summoned if they were needed by the government.

FACT

Loading and firing a flintlock musket has about 10 steps, including pouring measured powder, loading a cartridge, loading a ball, ramming the ball and powder, and firing. An expert soldier could fire up to four rounds per minute.

But despite this history, American scholars and historians have argued over the meaning and intent of the Second Amendment for more than 200 years. Some believe the intent of the amendment was to protect individual rights. Others believe the amendment was really addressing the role of states versus the federal government. In the past, some have argued that the amendment only applies to state militias, not to individual citizens.

For many who support what is often called "gun rights," the Second Amendment is a clear, firm statement. It protects the rights of individual citizens to own guns with little or no federal or state interference. Yet the First Amendment, which protects free speech, has plenty of restrictions. People are not allowed to incite violence with their speech, for instance, or use hate speech. So why should the Second Amendment be relatively free from such restrictions?

Female pro-gun activists marched as counterprotesters against the Million Mom March, a major rally for gun safety, on May 14, 2000, in Washington, D.C.

For people who demand far stricter gun control, the Second Amendment is complicated and possibly outdated. It was written at a time of muzzle-loading flintlock muskets that could shoot about three rounds per minute. Some people believe that in a world of semiautomatic weapons and handguns, the Second Amendment should apply only to militias, such as the National Guard.

Not All Random Violence Happens with Guns

Sometimes attacks in other countries are carried out with weapons other than guns, such as knives. Knives cannot kill as quickly or as effectively as guns, so the death toll tends to be lower. In 2018 Ichiro Kojima attacked three passengers on a Japanese bullet train traveling from Tokyo to Osaka. He stabbed all three with his knife, seriously injuring the two women and killing the man. And not all mass violence in the U.S. happens with guns. In July 2018 Timothy Kinner attacked a birthday party attended by Syrian and Iranian refugees in Boise, Idaho. He stabbed nine people, killing the three-year-old birthday girl.

In 2018 Mark Conditt incited panic when he mailed bombs randomly to African American targets. The bombs would explode when the package was opened or picked up. He killed two people before killing himself as police closed in. Kinner's and Conditt's attacks were racially motivated, so some would argue that they should be classified as terrorism. Mass violent attacks certainly occur outside the U.S., with or without guns. But the most violent mass attacks in the U.S. are committed by people armed with guns.

Guns and the Law

The first federal laws controlling gun ownership and use were passed in 1934. The National Firearms Act, signed into law by President Franklin Roosevelt, tried to control the guns used by organized crime and in gang activities. In 1993 President Bill Clinton signed the Brady Handgun Violence Prevention Act, which instituted background checks for citizens buying guns. The law came about after the 1981 attempted assassination of Ronald Reagan, and the injury of his press secretary, Jim Brady. In 1994 assault weapons were banned federally for 10 years. But after the ban expired in 2004, it was not renewed. As of 2019 assault weapons are permitted or banned state by state.

In 1997 President Bill Clinton signed into law a bill that prohibited foreigners from purchasing a handgun on visits to the United States. Jim Brady (right) and his wife, Sarah, looked on.

Federal laws have been enacted that protect gun dealers and manufacturers, and consequently, private gun owners. The Department of Justice appropriations bills include language from the Tiahrt Amendments, passed in 2003. These amendments shield gun sellers from public examination, lawsuits, and academic study. They do so by preventing the Bureau of Alcohol, Tobacco, and Firearms from releasing data saying where criminals bought their guns. In 2005 President George W. Bush signed a bill into law that prevented gun manufacturers from being sued by victims who were shot by guns made by that manufacturer.

State laws vary widely. Most states have some gun control laws on their books. The mass shooting at Marjory Stoneman Douglas High sparked more than 50 new regulations in various states in 2018. This was seen as a major victory for those who want more gun control. The federal government banned a device called a "bump stock." This attaches to a gun and converts it from a semiautomatic weapon, which is legal, to a fully automatic weapon, which is not. The ban was challenged in court

A bump stock attached to a semiautomatic weapon dramatically increases the firing rate.

by gun rights groups but the challenge failed. Other states passed what are called "red flag" laws, in which police can take away a citizen's guns if family or others suspect the person of becoming violent.

Ten states, however, increased gun rights laws, protecting gun owners who want to defend their homes with guns, for instance, or who want to allow people to carry guns in elementary, middle, and high schools. Mississippi, Missouri, Kansas, Arizona, Wyoming, and Idaho are the states with the least amount of gun control legislation. On the opposite end, California, New Jersey, Connecticut, Massachusetts, Maryland, and New York have the strictest gun laws in the country.

After every mass shooting, gun rights supporters and gun control advocates seem to rally in equal measure.

From 1983 to 2013, the U.S. had 78 mass shootings. That's more than any country in the world. Germany came in second—with seven. In 24 other industrialized countries, there were 41 total mass shootings among all of them. Scientists match this rate of mass shootings with the rate of gun ownership—countries with more guns also have high rates of mass shootings.

Shooting in Norway

The U.S. is not the only country to have experienced gun violence. Lisa Marie Husby survived the attack by Anders Behring Breivik on a Norwegian summer camp in 2011. She described the shooting in an October 19, 2017, interview with the UK's national network, the BBC. The following text is excerpted from that interview:

"I heard what I thought were fireworks. . . . Everyone was in shock at first, and I think we thought this is a horrible joke, this is too early to try and scare us. But then I realized seeing everyone who actually saw the gunman fleeing, that this was actually not a joke. . . . A lot of the people who actually saw what happened were fleeing, but this group were sheltered and they couldn't see what was happening, so they were just standing there not knowing what to do . . . there was so many gunshots because of the automatic gun he was using, so we thought there was more than one shooter. . . . We just hid under beds and tried to get into the small rooms inside the cabin and shelter ourselves from what was going on outside. We could hear the gunshots getting closer and further away and then suddenly they were very close."

After Columbine

After the tragedy at Columbine High School, people became more aware of the fact that kids had guns they could not have purchased legally. And kids were shooting each other. Some shooters were sad and angry. Some felt alienated from their classmates. There is no one reason why. But the shootings continue.

Columbine has spawned "copycat" attacks. Young killers express admiration for Harris and Klebold and model themselves after them. Columbine permanently changed how the police and the FBI respond to active shooter situations. Before Columbine, police would wait and set up a secure perimeter before going into a school. That's what happened at Columbine. Now, police and FBI are supposed to go straight in, toward the sound of guns, fast. Sometimes that still doesn't happen. During the MSD shooting, an armed security guard remained outside the school even though he was aware the shooting was happening. Authorities speculated that if he had gone in, he might have been able to save lives.

How were kids getting these guns? For the most part, they were taking them from their parents' homes. The *Washington Post* reports that in 80 percent of the 105 school shootings committed by minors in which the weapon's source was identified, the shooters had taken their parents', friends', or relatives' guns. Some might argue that the solution is fewer guns in people's homes. Others might say that the solution is better gun storage.

Another turning point came on December 14, 2012, when 20-year-old Adam Lanza burst into the Sandy Hook Elementary School in Newtown, Connecticut. He shot 20 first graders and six adult staff members. Sandy Hook stood out. The children were very young. Most other school shootings had happened in high schools. And the number of children murdered was very high. Lanza was isolated and troubled. He took guns from his mother's home and shot and killed her before driving to the school.

People in Newtown created a memorial to honor the 26 people killed at Sandy Hook Elementary School on December 14, 2012.

The violent murder of such very young children shook many in the nation. And Sandy Hook did change some parts of the gun debate. More money was funneled to gun control organizations. With those added funds, parents were able to organize on social media to advocate for gun control. But in an interview with *Time* magazine, Second Amendment expert Saul Cornell explains, "After Sandy Hook, America basically moved in two opposite directions at the state level. Places that had relatively weak gun-control regimes made them weaker, and places that had relatively strong gun-control regimes made them stronger." The opposite sides of the gun debate were strengthened, rather than coming together.

CHAPTER THREE

Gun **Control** and Gun **Rights**

[I] *heard a distinct "Pop! Pop! Pop! Pop!" I thought it was the sound guy messing up, but you learn quickly it's actual gunfire. . . . I just stood there. I didn't know what to do. Then I got on the ground. Every time it stopped, people would get up and start running. At this point, you have a mad rush of people running toward you. People hit the ground and jumped over things. It was a crowd of running people, you couldn't see anything. . . . I am just numb right now. It won't hit me till I get home and see my family.*

Justin Zimmerman, survivor of the
Route 91 Harvest Festival Las Vegas shooting

Since 2009 there have been 288 school shootings in the U.S. These shootings were not all mass shootings of the type defined by the FBI. Some of these shootings were related to gang violence or domestic violence. Some shootings were accidental. In some school shootings, only one person was killed. Others were mass shootings. But every one of those 288 shootings took a person's life. They occurred in Florida, Texas, California, Missouri, Maryland, Alabama, Michigan, Mississippi, and Virginia. But this list is by no means complete. In total, 39 states had at least one school shooting. The country with the next highest level of school shootings was Mexico, with eight.

Eighteen-year-old Sabika Sheikh was killed at Santa Fe High School in Galveston County, Texas, on May 18, 2018, by a student on the school's football team who was armed with two guns that belonged to his father. He began shooting in a first-period art class. In the end, 10 people were killed and 10 injured. Fourteen-year-old Alania Petty was killed at Marjory Stoneman Douglas High School in Parkland, Florida, by an active shooter who had been expelled from the school. He roamed the hallways, shooting at random and eventually killing 17 people and

> **FACT**
>
> Mass shootings can happen anywhere. Nine people were killed at the Emanuel African Methodist Episcopal Church in Charleston, South Carolina, by Dylann Roof, a white supremacist. Forty-nine people were killed at the Pulse Nightclub in Orlando, Florida. Fifty-eight people were killed at the Route 91 Harvest music festival in Las Vegas, Nevada. Nine people were killed at Umpqua Community College in Roseburg, Oregon.

injuring another 17. Jessica Rekos was only six years old when a gunman killed her and 25 others at the Sandy Hook Elementary School.

Though mass shootings can happen anywhere, school shootings feel particularly disturbing. In school shootings, the people who are shot and killed are children—the very people society tries hardest to protect. Schools are self-contained units. People entering and leaving are looked at more carefully than in other places. Schools are seen as both private, secure places and public, open places. And schools are trying to figure out how best to protect their students. In the 1950s people lived in fear of a nuclear attack from the Soviet Union (now Russia). Schools would hold "duck and cover" drills, in which students would be directed to hide under their desks. Students today would not recognize these drills. But they are probably familiar with lockdown drills. These are practice sessions in which schools act as if it is an active shooter situation.

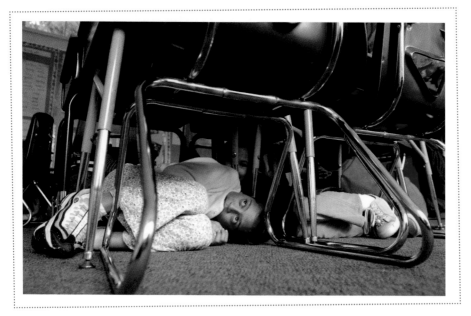

Elementary school students now regularly take part in lockdown drills.

The specifics of the drills vary. Usually, students and their teachers will lock the door of their classrooms, turn out the lights, and hide. Students might hide in bathrooms or in the teacher's lounge. Everyone stays away from the windows and doors. Some experts have recommended that schools use a system called ALICE: Alert, Lockdown, Inform, Counter, and Evacuate. The ALICE system has students and teachers use noise and movement to distract shooters and keep them from targeting specific victims. But other experts say that this system could not realistically prevent a shooter from killing or injuring students.

Some schools have chosen to add metal detectors, armed security officers, surveillance cameras, and secure entrances in which school doors are locked and visitors must be buzzed in. Some schools have added more staff dedicated to the students' mental health in an attempt to identify students who might commit shootings.

And a small number of school districts have chosen to arm teachers and staff with guns. That's by far the most controversial idea to

Metal detectors are used at school entrances to protect against guns.

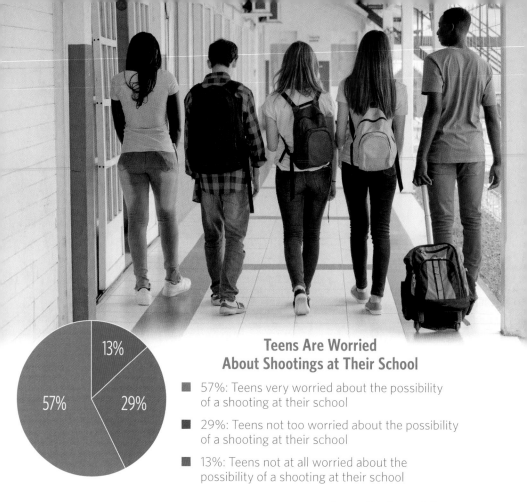

Teens Are Worried About Shootings at Their School

- 57%: Teens very worried about the possibility of a shooting at their school
- 29%: Teens not too worried about the possibility of a shooting at their school
- 13%: Teens not at all worried about the possibility of a shooting at their school

Source: Pew Research Center

protect students from school shootings. It is pushed by the Trump administration and the National Rifle Association (NRA). Lee County Public Schools in Virginia, for instance, has armed a small group of teachers and staff with Glock pistols. The armed teachers and staff have been trained by the local sheriff's department.

No one wants mass shooters. No one is on the side of killers. So you might think that there would be no argument about the role of guns in the U.S. and their relationship to mass shootings. Killing people is wrong. Guns are used to kill people. So should we take away guns?

Which side are you on?

The public discussion of the problem of mass shootings generally breaks down into two broad camps. One side wants gun control—fewer guns accessible to the public and more restrictions on who can buy guns, how, where, what type, and when. This side is often called "gun control advocates." The other side does not believe more gun control will solve the problem. This side believes that guns help keep people safer. They argue that gun ownership is an American right, and easy access to guns is protected by the U.S. Constitution. They say mass public and school shootings will not be prevented by restricting access to guns. This side is often called "gun rights advocates."

"A well regulated Militia, being necessary to the security of a free State, the right of the people to keep and bear Arms, shall not be infringed."

— Second Amendment to the U.S. Constitution

Background checks are not required for private gun sales in Louisiana.

Many gun control advocates argue that they do not want to take away guns from civilians in the U.S. So what do gun control advocates want? Fewer guns in the hands of fewer people. Gun control advocates often focus on background checks. When a person buys a gun, a federally licensed firearms dealer will check a person's history in an FBI database to see if that person has committed a crime or violence with a gun. But the background check laws are full of holes. Sales at gun shows aren't subject to background checks. In many states, these checks are not required for private sales. And not all crimes committed by people are listed in the database. Tightening up these holes will make background checks more effective, gun control advocates argue. Many kids who commit school shootings use guns already in their homes. So perhaps background checks would allow fewer parents to have guns.

Gun control advocates also argue for bans on certain types of guns—mainly assault weapons. An assault weapon is usually defined as the type of weapon the military might use, which can fire multiple rounds per trigger pull. These guns can be particularly deadly and advocates argue there is no reason for civilians to own them. They should be reserved for the military. And indeed, automatic weapons—machine guns—are banned in the U.S.

But gun control advocates and gun rights advocates argue fiercely over the restrictions of other assault weapons. Several mass shooters have used one particular kind of weapon, called the AR-15. The AR-15 is semiautomatic. That means a bullet is automatically loaded into the chamber ready for firing as soon as the previous bullet is fired. Semiautomatic weapons are sometimes permitted and sometimes banned, depending on the state.

AR-15s are a particular concern of gun control advocates as they can fire so many rounds without reloading.

Many argue that semiautomatic assault-style weapons should be banned entirely. At Columbine, Klebold and Harris used many kinds of guns, including semiautomatic guns. Lanza used a semiautomatic rifle at Sandy Hook. Cruz used a semiautomatic assault weapon at Marjory Stoneman Douglas.

Owning a gun is an American right, gun rights advocates argue. Guns are not used only to kill innocent people. Guns can be for self-protection, for sport, such as target shooting, and for hunting. In particular, hunting and sport shooting are part of some people's way of life and are important cultural activities for many people. Even more importantly, many gun rights advocates argue that armed civilians could help fight off attackers like mass shooters, thus making society safer. Some—including President Trump—have argued that arming teachers or having firearms on campus would be helpful.

Even some parents of school shooting victims and survivors agree. Fred Abt, whose child lived through the Marjory Stoneman Douglas shooting, told CNN, "One possible solution, which may not be very popular, would be to have people in the school, teachers, administrators who have volunteered to have a firearm safely locked in the classroom who are given training throughout the year. . . . There are plenty of teachers who are already licensed to carry firearms, have them raise their hands to volunteer for the training, and when something like this starts, the first responders are already on campus."

A program called FASTER gives teachers and school administrators training in responding to school violence.

Many children and teens are taught to hunt at an early age (above). Clay target shooting teams in high schools (below) are among the fastest growing sports in some parts of the U.S.

Other Forms of Gun Violence

Many people are shot in the U.S. every day, and for many reasons. People who commit domestic violence might shoot a girlfriend, wife, boyfriend, or husband. People kill each other in arguments over money, drugs, or property. And people have become more aware of the ways in which police and other law enforcement use their weapons. Black men are more likely to be shot by police—young black men, in particular. Many groups have argued that these shootings are motivated by racial prejudice, fear, and stereotyping rather than actual danger to officers' lives. The Black Lives Matter grassroots movement was born out of these concerns.

At a RiseUp rally in October 2015, more than 1,000 Black Lives Matter activists and supporters marched in support of the families of victims of alleged police brutality.

The Power of the
National Rifle Association

Gun rights advocates and their arguments are entwined
with that of a specific group—the National Rifle
Association (NRA). The NRA's goal is to influence
legislators to support policies favorable to gun rights.
The NRA is a powerful and well-known lobbying group
with an estimated 5 million members across the country.
The group originally focused on gun sports, like target
shooting, and on hunting. But over the years since its 1871
founding, and especially in the past few decades, the NRA
has become much more focused on the politics of gun
ownership. The organization exerts a lot of influence over

For decades, Wayne LaPierre has been a very effective spokesman for the
National Rifle Assocation.

members of Congress. In 2016 the NRA spent an estimated $54 million to elect members of Congress and a president who would support its goals. The NRA empowers its political action committee to rate members of Congress on a scale of A through F. Gun rights advocates listen to the words of the NRA leaders and consider them when voting on gun laws.

Despite the often bitter debate on both sides, there are some areas of overlap. Based on surveys of the general public, there is strong support for expanded background checks. That is, checking the background of people more thoroughly and consistently before allowing them to buy guns. And a vast majority of people also agree that guns should be kept out of the hands of people with mental illness. They support laws that would do so. But these changes are not supported by the NRA or by a majority in the U.S. Senate.

It's not clear how Americans are going to prevent mass killings like those at the Marjory Stoneman Douglas High School. Americans have been arguing about gun violence for a long time. But younger people have decided the debate is going too slowly for them. They're angry and they're not afraid to be angry and confrontational in public. In the days after the MSD shooting, many of the survivors declared their anger on social media.

To a Twitter user who said the MSD shooting was about a "lunatic," not guns, MSD student Carly Novell wrote, "I was hiding in a closet for 2 hours. It was about guns. You weren't there, you don't know how it felt. Guns give these disgusting people the ability to kill other human beings. This IS about guns and this is about all the people who had their life abruptly ended because of guns."

Student Kyra Parrow wrote, "A gun has killed 17 of my fellow classmates. A gun has traumatized my friends. My entire school, traumatized from this tragedy. This could have been prevented. . . ."

American Youth and Gun Violence Deaths

United States
vs.
Other High-Income Countries

Children ages 5–14:
14 times more likely
to be killed with guns in the U.S.

Teenagers:
23 times more likely
to be killed with guns in the U.S.

Source: https://everytownresearch.org/impact-gun-violence-american-children-teens/

CHAPTER FOUR

#NeverAgain
Rises Up

*P*opping sounds, like those of a balloon bursting, erupted seemingly behind the building. . . . I didn't know what possessed me to do it, but I bolted into the building. . . . I made it to the second floor of the building. . . . Gunpowder choked the hallway into submission. . . . I sprinted to the boys' bathroom and charged for the largest stall. . . . I heard everything. I could only hope the noise was coming from thirty textbooks being dropped at the same time—each one closer to the bathroom. I didn't know where the shots were coming from. I didn't know if the shooter was in the hallway right outside the bathroom or on the third floor above me. I didn't know if death would follow me to the stall. I didn't know anything.

Andy Pedroza, survivor of the
Marjory Stoneman Douglas High School shooting

Something changed in the students at Marjory Stoneman Douglas High after the shooting at their school on February 14, 2018. One day later they decided they were done waiting for something to be done, somewhere, about mass shootings and gun violence. They were going to do something themselves. A small group of student activists formed what soon became known as #NeverAgain. The movement is more than just a hashtag. It is a student-led, grassroots social movement. Its leaders have spoken at gun control rallies, written editorials, and appeared on CNN, other networks, and late-night TV shows. Again and again, they have said that young people are fed up with lawmakers' unwillingness to pass meaningful gun control laws. "We've had enough," MSD senior Ryan Diestch said during an interview with PBS News. "We are the

A week after the shooting at Marjory Stoneman Douglas, students from the school, along with thousands of others, gathered at the state capitol in Florida to protest the state's loose gun laws.

generation that was born after Columbine. We have lived with [this] our entire lives and now it happened at my school. I spent two hours in a closet just hiding and I am done hiding. We're done hiding. America has done hiding."

The #NeverAgain organizers, all teenagers, began working with other groups and political leaders to organize the March for Our Lives. This first march and rally took place on March 24, 2018. Its mission statement was simple: "Not one more. We cannot allow one more child to be shot at school." The organizers wanted to be particularly clear that the rally was not political. #NeverAgain was intended to be nonpartisan. It was about life and safety. These were goals on which the movement hoped everyone could agree.

Students led the March for Our Lives demonstration in March 2018.

"Six Minutes and About 20 Seconds"

Emma Gonzalez Speaks at March for Our Lives

MSD shooting survivor Emma Gonzalez spoke powerfully at the March for Our Lives rally in Washington, D.C. Her speech helped identify her as one of the leaders of the #NeverAgain movement.

"Six minutes, and about 20 seconds. In a little over six minutes, 17 of our friends were taken from us, . . . more were injured, and everyone, absolutely everyone in the Douglas community was forever altered. Everyone who was there understands. Everyone who has been touched by the cold grip of gun violence understands. For us, long, tearful, chaotic hours in the scorching afternoon sun were spent not knowing.

"No one understood the extent of what had happened. No one could believe that there were bodies in that building waiting to be identified for over a day. No one knew that the people who were missing had stopped breathing long before any of us had even known that a code red had been called. No one could comprehend the devastating aftermath, or how far this would reach, or where this would go."

The movement, anchored by the marches, took off, perhaps because it was organized and led by the very people affected by school shootings—not by politicians or civic leaders. News organizations like CBS estimated that 200,000 people attended the main march in Washington.

Organizers of the march estimated that 800,000 attended. This is a big difference, but no matter which number is more accurate, that attendance was massive. And thousands of

FACT

Even the lower estimate of 200,000 attendees at the March for Our Lives on March 24, 2018, puts it on par with the largest marches and demonstrations in U.S. history. The 1963 March on Washington for Jobs and Freedom had 250,000 attendees. The 2017 Women's March had 500,000 attendees.

others marched in cities around the country. "Welcome to the revolution," MSD student Cameron Kasky told the crowd in Washington, D.C. Speakers talked about mass shootings, but also about gun violence in general. Speakers noted that black children are shot at a rate 10 times that of white children.

People of all ages participated in the nationwide March for Our Lives rally in March 2018. Among them were these Los Angeles students.

Gun control social media campaigns after mass shootings are not new. Others have used Twitter and other social media platforms to express themselves after a shooting and to call for stricter gun laws. Researchers studying these communications have found that they tend to die out after a certain period of time. They've found that these social media campaigns haven't changed gun laws.

On the other hand, gun rights advocates waged steady social media campaigns after mass shootings, citing the Second Amendment and arguing against restricting guns. These gun rights campaigns tended to continue after the gun control social media campaigns faded away.

But #NeverAgain may be different. The leaders have shown that they are willing to engage aggressively and directly on social media. They've kept the conversation going long after the shooting at MSD. "Articulate, witty and digitally native, the survivors of the school shooting in Parkland, Florida, are using social media to debunk conspiracy theories and amplify their voices in a way the world hasn't seen before. With thoughtful tweets about gun control, a fearlessness for taking on politicians and sharply worded messages to shut down conspiracy theorists, the students of Marjory Stoneman Douglas High School are leading a movement," wrote journalist Alyssa Newcomb on NBCNews.com.

David Hogg (center, holding mic) became a leading spokesman for the #NeverAgain movement. For this, he was called a "crisis actor" by conspiracy theorists.

And this movement has led to real change. Inspired at least in part by the teenagers leading the #NeverAgain movement, state lawmakers across the country passed broad changes to the gun laws. Vermont banned guns in K–12 schools. Oklahoma further restricted who can carry a concealed weapon. Tennessee expanded background checks. And the Trump administration's Justice Department is reclassifying bump stocks as machine guns and banning them under the laws already on the books.

> **FACT**
>
> Eighty-six percent of teens surveyed by the Pew Research Center said that preventing people with mental illness from purchasing guns would be an effective gun control measure. About 39 percent of teens surveyed said that allowing teachers to carry guns would be somewhat or very effective.

Gun control advocates and the leaders of #NeverAgain have not won all the victories. Since the MSD shooting, 10 states have passed laws that favor gun rights. Some states now permit arming teachers with guns. Others allowed broader definitions for gun self-defense laws, often called "stand-your-ground" laws. But #NeverAgain has achieved at least some of its goals—real, practical change to gun laws. And the group is still working. The organizers continue to speak out in person and on social media. The group maintains an active website full of information about gun control and has recently focused heavily on encouraging young people to vote.

CHAPTER FIVE

What Happens
After a Shooting?

It is hard to believe that all of this has happened in the same calendar year. From our lives as normal high school students, to activists born of tragedy, to caricatures of the gun lobby and many of their supporters, 2018 has changed our lives forever and set us on a path to effect sane gun laws for America once and for all.

The shooting at our school also sent me and my friends on a journey into the heart of our country, and on this journey we have discovered that Americans are more divided than ever before. These divisions are exploited and encouraged by those at the top, the people we once called "leaders," who are supposed to make our democracy function, smooth over our differences, and lead us toward solutions to our problems. Instead, our "leaders" too often have us at each other's throats and encourage us to think *the very worst of each other, which only hardens positions and hearts, reinforces biases, and closes minds and ears. . . . This is the world we are trying to change.*

David Hogg, survivor of the
Marjory Stoneman Douglas High shooting

What happens after a shooting? An MSD student recalls being picked up by his dad. He went home and sat at the table with his mom, trying to eat lunch. The experience felt unreal. How can you be normal after something like that? How does it feel to enter your school after a shooting? What thoughts come to you at night? What about when you hear a loud noise? Or when you want to call your friend, and you remember she's dead?

About 28 percent of people who have been in a mass shooting develop post-traumatic stress disorder (PTSD). About a third of people develop acute stress disorder. These mental health problems are the result of the trauma of having seen such violence. Mass shootings are particularly upsetting to survivors because they're random, happen without warning, and in places people believe themselves to be safe, like their school or their church, according to the American Psychological Assocation. People feel shock, disbelief, and fear. Later, they often feel anger, anxiety, and depression. They may have difficulty sleeping or paying attention when awake.

Getting help and staying connected are essential to dealing with the trauma of a mass shooting, and eventually, feeling better. Psychologists have found that the people who do the best after mass violence are those who feel connected to their broader community and who have support available to them. Attending vigils and memorials can be very helpful, as well as going to support groups and talking with therapists. A community event in which people come together to acknowledge what happened can be very helpful to survivors, psychologists have found. Likewise, research shows that when people simply know counseling is available, even if they don't use it, they feel better. Feeling connected to others is essential to combat the trauma that comes with mass violence. Teachers and administrators might need special training to help kids who have been through a school shooting.

"Every gunshot I heard was the sound of my brain going deeper and deeper into a shock. My body was there, under a table, fearing for my life. But my mind was still in my desk, next to the door, laughing with Alyssa. I look at my friend. And within seconds, Alyssa is struck with bullets. She is dying. My friend, who I was talking with two minutes before, is dying."

— Eden Hebron, survivor of the MSD shooting

Talking about trauma with those who have experienced it, as well as with a counselor, has been found to be helpful.

Recovering can take a long time—months or even years. Some people might only need counseling for a few months. But others might need it much longer. People who were physically closer to a mass shooting, who were shot themselves, or who saw people shot, tend to have more PTSD symptoms than people who were not as directly connected to the mass shooting.

Signs and Symptoms of PTSD

Signs of Intrusive Memories
• Recurring memories of the traumatic event
• Flashbacks of the traumatic event
• Nightmares of the traumatic event

Signs of Avoidance
• Trying to avoid thinking or talking about the traumatic event
• Trying to avoid people and places that remind you of the traumatic event

Signs of Negative Thinking or Mood
• Negative thoughts about yourself or the world
• Hopelessness in relation to the future
• Not remembering parts of the traumatic event
• Feeling numb or detached
• Lack of interest in activities

Signs of Changes in Emotional and Physical Reactions
• Trouble sleeping
• Trouble concentrating
• Having outbursts of anger
• Feeling overwhelming guilt
• Being easily startled or frightened

Source: "Post-Traumatic Stress Disorder."
Mayo Clinic. www.mayoclinic.org/diseases-conditions/post-traumatic-stress-disorder/symptoms-causes/syc-20355967

In March 2019 two students who had lived through the MSD shooting and a father of a child killed in the Sandy Hook shooting died by suicide. No one can say that living through these traumatic events caused these deaths. But intense guilt over having lived through a shooting while others died is not uncommon. Survivors might feel that they should have done something to save their friends or children or that the shooting was somehow their fault.

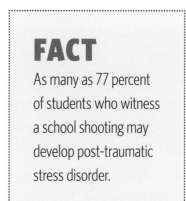

FACT

As many as 77 percent of students who witness a school shooting may develop post-traumatic stress disorder.

Connecting with other survivors can help. Students who have been through a mass school shooting often have an instant connection. In May 2018, MSD shooting survivor Eden Hebron wrote a letter, published in *USA Today*, to survivors of a school shooting in Santa Fe, Texas. "Everyone says, 'I can't imagine,'" she wrote. "But, this time, I can. I can imagine what it's like to go through something that you never thought you'd have to. To question if you were going to make it home that day. And I am here in Parkland, Fla., a student who watched three lives taken from this world, to tell you that you are going to be OK. Not tomorrow, not next week, but eventually, you will be OK."

For some students, taking action can be part of healing. Joining and working in a movement like #NeverAgain can help survivors feel that they are not helpless and not victims. They are working toward a goal with others who understand what they've been through. Researching the gun control laws in one's own school district and city can be a good way to take action. Students can form a small group to draw up a list of requests for the school board or city council. Then they can present their requests at the next school board or city council meeting that is open to the public. In 2017 the city council of the small town of Wyoming, Ohio, passed a measure allowing concealed weapons in city buildings. Citizens banded together, appeared at the city council meeting, and demanded that the measure be repealed. After listening to the citizens, the council changed the policy. The citizens had a real effect on the presence of guns in their immediate local community.

In many different ways, guns are a part of American life. For some, they are dangerous, uncontrolled weapons that kill innocent people. For others, they are proud symbols of rural life, heritage, and independence. Many Americans question the nation's gun laws. The laws are constantly being debated. No American wants to see innocent people killed in mass shootings. The question of whether more guns, fewer guns, and what kind of guns will stop active shooters is far from resolved. But #NeverAgain and the youth gun movement have galvanized young people in this country. The future of gun control will likely be determined by them.

Black Lives Matter

Mass shootings are far from the only type of gun violence in the U.S. Black people are 10 times more likely to die of gun violence than white people. After the death of black teenager Trayvon Martin in 2012, his shooter, a white man named George Zimmerman, was acquitted of the charges of second-degree murder and manslaughter. The grassroots movement Black Lives Matter was organized soon after. Its purpose was to bring attention to the anger and frustration that many in the black community felt at what they saw as black lives being valued less than white lives. The movement drew attention to the problem of police shootings of black men and teenagers. In 2014 demonstrations were held across the country when two unarmed black men, Michael Brown and Eric Garner, were killed by police. Black Lives Matter has continued to work for fair treatment for black men and teenagers at the hands of police.

In 2012 thousands rallied in Florida to show support for Trayvon Martin's family. Civil rights activist Jesse Jackson (third from left) marched at the front with Al Sharpton (center) and NAACP President Ben Jealous (center, right).

GET INVOLVED

Here's what you can do to help combat gun violence and mass shootings.

Research the gun laws in your state and city. If gun legislation is coming up for a vote or about to be vetoed or signed into law, take note of when.

Then, write, call, or visit your congressional representative and your senators. Prepare talking points in advance stating your name, age, where you live, and exactly what you want your representative or your senators to know. If a specific piece of legislation is coming up for a vote, tell your representative or senators how you want them to vote.

Join a chapter of an advocacy group in your area. Attend a rally or a meeting to see if the group and its goals are a good fit.

Research changes you would like to see at your own school that could help protect against future gun violence. How can your school be a safer place? Talk to your friends, write up a list of requests, then organize a group of students to attend the next meeting of the school board. Be ready to present your demands and your reasons.

Attend a rally, vigil, or memorial for victims of gun violence if one is being held in your area. Even if you weren't specifically connected to the shooting, going to the community event can help you feel connected and safe.

GLOSSARY

acute stress disorder—an anxiety condition characterized by amnesia, feelings of numbness, feeling like your thoughts don't belong to you, feeling like your surroundings aren't real, flashbacks, and nightmares. ASD typically occurs within a month after a traumatic event and lasts at least three days

advocates—people who publicly support a particular cause or position

appropriations—money set aside by a formal action or for a specific use

industrialized—characterized by having a developed economy and an advanced technological infrastructure

lobbying group—a group that tries to influence public opinion or policy, sometimes by attempting to influence the votes of lawmakers

post-traumatic stress disorder—a condition of mental and emotional stress that can occur after a traumatic event. PTSD often involves having trouble sleeping and repeated mental images of the traumatic event, combined with a feeling of dullness to the rest of the world

statistics—the practice of collecting and analyzing data in large quantities

trauma—an emotional upset from a horrifying event

ADDITIONAL RESOURCES

Critical Thinking Questions

Gun rights advocates and gun control advocates disagree on how guns should be regulated and controlled in the United States. Using the text, summarize both arguments. Then state your own opinion.

The NRA seeks to change or uphold gun laws by lobbying members of Congress. The #NeverAgain movement has tried to change gun laws by using social media and holding rallies. Do you think these methods are effective? Which are the most and least effective and why?

The final chapter of this book discusses what can help survivors of a school shooting. Read over the text. Now write three additional suggestions of your own.

Further Reading

Falkowski, Melissa, and Eric Garner, eds. *We Say Never Again: Reporting by the Parkland Student Journalists.* New York: Crown, 2018.

Hogg, David, and Lauren Hogg. *#NeverAgain: A New Generation Draws the Line.* New York: Random House, 2018.

Lerner, Sarah. *Parkland Speaks: Survivors from Marjory Stoneman Douglas Share Their Stories.* New York: Crown, 2019.

March for Our Lives Action Fund. *Glimmer of Hope: How a Tragedy Sparked a Movement.* New York: Penguin, 2018.

Internet Sites

Everytown for Gun Safety
https://everytownresearch.org/

Kids Health: Gun Safety
https://kidshealth.org/en/kids/gun-safety.html

March for Our Lives
https://marchforourlives.com/

SOURCE NOTES

p. 4, "I've never had a great memory…" Melissa Falkowski and Eric Garner, eds. *We Say Never Again: Reporting by the Parkland Student Journalists*. New York: Crown, 2018.

p. 12, "A single loud bang…" Ibid.

p. 13, "For the first time in my life…" Nicole Pelletiere, "Inside Room 211: The Massacre at Virginia Tech Remembered 10 Years Later," ABC News, April 13, 2017, https://abcnews.go.com/US/room-211-massacre-virginia-tech-remembered-10-years/story?id=46701034 Accessed December 29, 2018.

p. 22, "I heard what I thought…""Norway Massacre: 'We Could Hear the Gunshots Getting Closer,'" BBC News, October 19, 2017, https://www.bbc.com/news/uk-scotland-41678010 Accessed January 9, 2019.

p. 25, "After Sandy Hook…" Olivia B. Waxman, "It's About Almost Anything But the Guns: Sandy Hook and the Originial Meaning of the Second Amendment," *Time*, December 14, 2017, http://time.com/5061579/sandy-hook-newtown-history/ Accessed January 25, 2019.

p. 26, "You heard a distinct…" Nation Now, "'Blood All Over the Elevator:' Las Vegas Shooting Survivors Recall Attack in Own Words," WBIR Channel 10 News, October 2, 2017, https://www.wbir.com/article/news/nation-now/blood-all-over-the-elevator-las-vegas-shooting-survivors-recall-attack-in-own-words/465-53ce37bb-0287-4592-9915-1e84bdad4f82 Accessed March 1, 2019.

p. 34, "One possible solution…" Dan Merica, and Betsy Klein, "Trump Suggests Arming Teachers as a Solution to Increase School Safety," CNN, February 22, 2018, https://www.cnn.com/2018/02/21/politics/trump-listening-sessions-parkland-students/index.html Accessed January 25, 2019.

p. 38, "I was hiding in a closet…" Robinson Meyer, "The Righteous Anger of the Parkland Shooting's Teen Survivors," *The Atlantic*, February 17, 2018, https://www.theatlantic.com/technology/archive/2018/02/parkland-shooting-teen-survivor-tweets-righteous-anger/553634/ Accessed January 25, 2019.

p. 39, "A gun has killed…" Ibid.

p. 40, "Popping sounds…" *We Say Never Again: Reporting by the Parkland Student Journalists*, pp. 145–146.

pp. 41–42,,"We've had enough…" Ibid.

p. 42, "Not one more…" Lauren Holter, "Who Organized the March For Our Lives? Never Again MSD Has a Heart-Wrenching Goal," *Bustle*, March 21, 2018, https://www.bustle.com/p/who-organized-the-march-for-our-lives-never-again-msd-has-a-heart-wrenching-goal-8563862 Accessed January 6, 2019.

p. 43, "Six minutes, and about 20 seconds…" Chris Tognotti, "Transcript of Emma Gonzalez March for Our Lives Speech Will Absolutely Crush You," *Bustle*, March 24, 2018, https://www.bustle.com/p/transcript-of-emma-gonzalezs-march-for-our-lives-speech-will-absolutely-crush-you-8596656 Accessed January 10, 2019.

p. 46, "Welcome to the revolution…" Ray Sanchez, "Student Marchers Call Washington's Inaction on Gun Violence Unacceptable," CNN, March 24, 2018, https://www.cnn.com/2018/03/24/us/march-for-our-lives/index.html Accessed January 6, 2019.

p. 47, "Articulate, witty and digitally native…" Alyssa Newcomb, "How Parkland's Social Media-Savvy Teens Took Back the Internet—and the Gun Control Debate," NBC News, February 22, 2018, https://www.nbcnews.com/tech/tech-news/how-parkland-students-are-using-social-media-keep-gun-control-n850251 Accessed January 6, 2019.

p. 49, "…it is hard to believe…" *We Say Never Again*, pp. 237–238.

p. 51, "Every gunshot I heard…" Eden Hebron, "Flashback: Here's What It Was Like to Watch My Friends Die in Room 1216," *USA Today*, April 5, 2018, https://www.usatoday.com/story/opinion/2018/04/05/parkland-school-shooting-survivor-watched-friends-die-column/487169002/ Accessed January 11, 2019.

p. 53, "Everyone says, 'I can't imagine…" Eden Hebron, "Dear Texas School Shooting Survivors: A Parkland Teen's Advice to Santa Fe Students," *USA Today*, May 20, 2018, https://www.usatoday.com/story/opinion/2018/05/20/santa-fe-texas-school-shooting-parkland-survivor-advice-column/627057002/ Accessed January 11, 2019.

SELECT BIBLIOGRAPHY

Books

Cook, Philip J., and Kristin A. Goss. *The Gun Debate: What Everyone Needs to Know.* New York: Oxford University Press, 2014.

Falkowski, Melissa, and Eric Garner, eds. *We Say Never Again: Reporting by the Parkland Student Journalists.* New York: Crown, 2018.

Klarevas, Louis. *Rampage Nation: Securing America From Mass Shootings.* Amherst, NY: Prometheus Books, 2016.

Websites and Articles

Allen, Greg, "Suicides in Parkland Leave Community in Shock," npr. org, March 25, 2019, https://www.npr.org/2019/03/25/706598774/ suicides-in-parkland-leave-community-in-shock Accessed March 27, 2019.

"Annual Gun Law Scorecard," Giffords Law Center, https://lawcenter. giffords.org/scorecard/ Accessed December 29, 2018.

Berkowitz, Bonnie, Denise Lu, and Chris Alcantara, "The Terrible Numbers That Grow With Each Mass Shooting," *Washington Post*, November 9, 2018, https://www.washingtonpost.com/ graphics/2018/national/mass-shootings-in-america/?noredirect=on&utm_term=.30fffbfd5a15 Accessed December 29, 2018.

Carlsen, Audrey, and Sahil Chinoy March, "How to Buy a Gun in 15 Countries," *The New York Times*, March 2, 2018, https://www. nytimes.com/interactive/2018/03/02/world/international-gun-laws. html Accessed December 29, 2018.

Daniels, Jess, "Definition of What's Actually an 'Assault Weapon' Is a Highly Contentious Issue," CNBC, February 27, 2018, https://www. cnbc.com/2018/02/21/definition-of-whats-an-assault-weapon-is-a-very-contentious-issue.html Accessed December 29, 2018.

Duwe, Grant, "Mass Shootings Are Getting Deadlier, Not More Frequent," *Politico Magazine*, October 4, 2017, https://www.politico.com/ magazine/story/2017/10/04/mass-shootings-more-deadly-frequent-research-215678 Accessed December 29, 2018.

Gonsalves, Kelly, "America's Era of Duck-and-Cover," *The Week*, https://theweek.com/captured/722874/americas-era-duckandcover Accessed January 9, 2019.

Grabow, Chip, and Lisa Rose, "The U.S. Has Had 57 Times as Many School Shootings as Other Major Industrialized Nations Combined," CNN, May 21, 2018, https://www.cnn.com/2018/05/21/us/school-shooting-us-versus-world-trnd/index.html Accessed December 29, 2018.

Gray, Sarah, "Here's a Timeline of the Major Gun Control Laws in America," *Time*, February 22, 2018, http://time.com/5169210/us-gun-control-laws-history-timeline/ Accessed December 29, 2018.

"Gun Violence in America," Everytown for Gun Safety, January 4, 2019, https://everytownresearch.org/gun-violence-america/ Accessed January 11, 2019.

Kaste, Martin, "Despite Heightened Fear of School Shootings, It's Not a Growing Epidemic," NPR, March 15, 2018, https://www.npr.org/2018/03/15/593831564/the-disconnect-between-perceived-danger-in-u-s-schools-and-reality Accessed December 20, 2018.

Lemieux, Frederic, "6 Things to Know About Mass Shootings in America," *Scientific American*, June 13, 2016, https://www.scientificamerican.com/article/6-things-to-know-about-mass-shootings-in-america/ Accessed December 29, 2018.

Lund, Nelson, and Adam Winkler, "The Second Amendment," National Constitution Center, https://constitutioncenter.org/interactive-constitution/amendments/amendment-ii Accessed December 29, 2018.

"Mass Shootings: Definition and Trends," RAND Corporation, https://www.rand.org/research/gun-policy/analysis/supplementary/mass-shootings.html Accessed December 29, 2018.

Meyer, Robinson, "The Righteous Anger of the Parkland Shooting's Teen Survivors," *The Atlantic*, February 17, 2018, https://www.theatlantic.com/technology/archive/2018/02/parkland-shooting-teen-survivor-tweets-righteous-anger/553634/ Accessed January 25, 2019.

Novotney, Amy, "What Happens to the Survivors," *American Psychological Association*, September 8, 2018, https://www.apa.org/monitor/2018/09/survivors.aspx Accessed January 6, 2019.

Parker, Kim et al., "America's Complex Relationship with Guns," Pew Research Center, June 22, 2017, http://www.pewsocialtrends. org/2017/06/22/the-demographics-of-gun-ownership/ Accessed January 25, 2019.

Perez-Pena, Richard, "Gun Control Explained," *The New York Times*, October 7, 2015, https://www.nytimes.com/interactive/2015/10/07/us/ gun-control-explained.html Accessed January 6, 2019.

Rabinovich, Ben, "What Is the NRA and How Many Members Does It Have?" *Daily Mail*, February 22, 2018, https://www.dailymail.co.uk/ news/article-5422121/What-NRA-members-does-have.html Accessed January 9, 2019.

Sanchez, Ray, "How Columbine Changed the Way Police Respond to Mass Shootings," CNN, February 15, 2018, https://www.cnn. com/2018/02/15/us/florida-school-shooting-columbine-lessons/index. html Accessed January 9, 2019.

"Second Amendment," Legal Information Institute, https://www.law. cornell.edu/wex/second_amendment# Accessed December 29, 2018.

"The Impact of Gun Violence on American Children and Teenagers," Everytown for Gun Safety, August 15, 2018, https://everytown research.org/impact-gun-violence-american-children-teens/ Accessed January 10, 2019.

Vasilogambros, Matt, "After Parkland, States Pass 50 New Gun-Control Laws," Pew Trusts Stateline, August 2, 2018, https://www.pewtrusts. org/en/research-and-analysis/blogs/stateline/2018/08/02/after-parkland-states-pass-50-new-gun-control-laws Accessed December 29, 2018.

Waxman, Olivia B., "'It's About Almost Anything But the Guns: Sandy Hook and the Originial Meaning of the Second Amendment," *Time*, December 14, 2017, http://time.com/5061579/sandy-hook-newtown-history/ Accessed January 25, 2019.

Willingham, A.J., and Saeed Ahmed, "Mass Shootings in America Are a Serious Problem—And These 9 Charts Show Just Why," CNN, November 6, 2017, https://www.cnn.com/2016/06/13/health/mass-shootings-in-america-in-charts-and-graphs-trnd/index.html Accessed December 29, 2018.

Yuhas, Alan, "The Right to Bear Arms: What Does the Second Amendment Really Mean?" *The Guardian*, October 5, 2017, https://www. theguardian.com/us-news/2017/oct/05/second-amendment-right-to-bear-arms-meaning-history Accessed December 29, 2018.

About the Author

Emma Carlson Berne has written more than 90 books for children and young adults. She lives in Cincinnati, Ohio, with her husband and three little boys, ages 10, 7, and 3. When she's not writing, Emma rides horses, hikes, and reads books to her sons.

INDEX